The Hillbilly to English

why wait weeks?
speak fluent Hillbilly today!

100's
of
entries

also...

my
personal
favorite
Hillbilly
sayings

A 'Must Have' if
traveling down south!

a laugh on every page,
from cover to cover

By
Richard Nivens

In Loving Memory of my Mother
Brenda Faye Nivens
From Livingston Tennessee

You will find the entries here exactly like a collegiate dictionary, except different. Here is an example…

Dumb as a brick: *1. Phrase used to measure intelligence.*
HB: Bobby iz in the hospital and heez dumb as a brick.
ENG: I am sorry to inform you of this, your brother Robert is in a coma.

First you will find the hillbilly word and a translation. The word will then be shown in a hillbilly sentence marked "HB". You will then find a sentence with a close English translation marked "ENG".

The spelling on the hillbilly words are approximate. Nobody knows for sure how to spell the way they speak. The government is still doing research.

Many of the words are words that we use every day. They just seem to have an entirely different meaning in the southeastern region of our great country.

Agin: *(Again) 1. Against.*

HB: Ats agin da law.
ENG: That would violate the law.

After whall: *1. Later on. 2. After while.*
HB: All tend to it after whall.
ENG: I'll take care of it later.

Ahhitede *n: (AHH-ITE-DEN) 1. All right then. 2. OK.*
HB: Awiteden.
ENG: Ok, that's fine.

All: *1. I'll. 2. I will be.*
HB: All see ya after whall.
ENG: I'll see you later.

Argyen: *(ARG-YEN) 1. To argue.*
HB: What's all iss argyen about?
ENG: Why are you guys arguing?

Arz: *1. Ours.*
HB: Ya sure this un iz arz darlin?
ENG: Honey, our new baby looks just like the guy at the Chinese buffet Yen Chow. I shouldn't drive a truck out of town for two weeks at a time.

Ats: *1. That's. 2. That is.*
HB: Ats yers sweetpea.
ENG: Happy anniversary honey, I got you this fancy napkin from the bar.

Atta: *1. That.*
HB: Is em aire viddles atta way?
ENG: Where is the dining room?

Atti *n: 1. That one.*
HB: I like atin aire.

ENG: I like that one right there.

Attaway: 1. In that direction. 2. To move away from you.
HB: Push it over attaway Wilma.
ENG: Lets move the sofa to the other side of the room.

Barrellin: 1. To move quickly.
HB: I come barrellin when I heard at aire supper bell.
ENG: I came quickly when I heard you say dinner was ready.

Belly Ache: 1. To complain.
HB: All he did was belly ache all day.
ENG: He sure did complain a lot.

Bess: 1. Better. 2. Probably should.
HB: You bess get outside where ya belong.
ENG: You kids should play outside for a while.

Bigger fish ta fry: 1. Better things to do.
HB: I wuz throwin ma beer cans outa ma pickup winder when the sheriff happened along and kept a goin. I reckon he had bigger fish to fry.
ENG: Some litter accidentally blew out of my car window as the police passed me by. I suppose he had a more important call to respond to.

Bloody stub: 1. Severed appendage.
HB: Ya reach in at cooks winder and ya might draw back a bloody stub.
ENG: You grab that food and the cook might cut off your hand.

Boondoggle: 1. To use deception.
HB: Ed got boondoggled by the car guy.
ENG: Edwin was sold a lemon by the car dealer

Box a rocks: 1. Measurement used to determine someone's intelligence.
HB: Ole Billy iz dumb as a box a rocks.
ENG: William seems to be somewhat intellectually challenged.

Carters got pills: *1. Used to compare a certain amount of something.*
HB: Willis got more skeeter bites an carters got pills.
ENG: The doctor said William had more mosquito bites than he could count.
Carter may be a pharmaceutical company, I don't know

Cha   r: *1. Chair.*
HB: Reckon I'll sit in ma char fer a spell.
ENG: I think I'll sit in my new chair for a while.

Cook out: *1. Barbeque.*
HB: Sweetpea, lets have a cook out with at roadkill ya picked up.
ENG: Lets barbeque that meat you picked up today honey.

Commence: *1. To begin.*
HB: I'ze goin to commence workin right now.
ENG: You're 30 minutes late, you're fired.

Critters: *Animals. 2. Pets.*
HB: I got me sum critters over he'ahh.
ENG: I have several lovely pets at home.

Dagbur n: *1. Darn it. 2. Unknown word, hard to describe.*
HB: Dagburn it all.
ENG: This is to hard, I give up.

Directly: *1. Right away. 2. Soon. 3. Later on.*
HB: All be over directly.
ENG: OK, I am on my way.

Double quick: *1. To do something quickly.*
HB: All be over double quick.
ENG: I'll be right over.

Dumb as a brick: *1. Phrase used to measure intelligence.*
HB: Bobby iz in the hospital and heez dumb as a brick.
ENG: I am sorry to inform you of this, your brother Robert is in a coma.

Eez: *1. These.*
HB: Eez he'ahh fixins sho iz fine.
ENG: These new clothes are pretty nice.

Ears flappi   n: *1. To be hard of hearing.*
HB: Yer ears flappin son?
ENG: Can you hear me ok?

Earshot: *1. Nearby. 2. Within shouting distance.*
HB: Ma kin folk aint but an earshot away.
ENG: My family is nearby.

Em: *1. Them.*
HB: Em was some rite fine gizzards darlin.
ENG: Those chicken guts were pretty good honey.

E   r: *1. Or.*
HB: Ya want one a eez er one a the otherins?
ENG: Would you like one of these or one of the other ones?

Et: *1. Ate.*
HB: I done et ma supper.
ENG: I've finished my dinner.

Ever which way: *1. Encircled by. 2. In each direction.*
HB: Thays sum good fishin ever which way.
ENG: There are good fishing spots everywhere around here.

Fair: *1. Long (time, distance etc).*
HB: Ma car broke and I had ta walk a fair whall.
ENG: My car broke down and I had to walk for several miles.

Far: *1. Fire. 2. Extreme heat.*

HB: I feel like I'm on far.
ENG: It's very hot out today.

Fard: *1. Fired. 2. Released from employment.*
HB: Esther got fard from the plant.
ENG: Esther lost her job at the chicken rendering plant.

Favor: *1. To look like or be like.*
HB: Are kid favors at feller what mowed are grass last summer darlin.
ENG: You been messing around on me honey?

Fellers: *1. Two or more men.*
HB: Em aire fellers do good work.
ENG: The painters did a good job.

Fe   r: *1. For.*
HB: Whadja do at fer?
ENG: Why did you do that?

Fester: *1. Infected wound. 2. Wound seeping unknown fluids.*
HB: At cut on yer hand is startin ta fester.
ENG: I think your injury has become infected.

Fetch: *1. To get something.*
HB: I'ze fixin ta fetch me up sum viddles.
ENG: I am calling for Chinese take out.

Fiddle: *1. Violin.*
HB: Earl plays some knee slappin fiddle.
ENG: Earl is a talented violinist.

Fiddlin: *1. To mess around.*
HB: Yer jussa fiddlin around.
ENG: Quit messing around and finish your assignment.

Fixin: *1. Preparing. 2. Getting ready to.*
HB: I'ze fixin ta trim up the yard.

ENG: I am preparing to mow the lawn.

Fixins: *1. New clothes, mobile home etc.*
HB: My fixins wuz blowed away by a nader.
ENG: The local trailer park was leveled by a tornado.

Flap Jacks: *1. Pancakes.*
HB: My ma makes some rite fine flap jacks.
ENG: My Mothers pancakes are delectable.

Flimflammer: *1. Word used to describe an unknown object.*
HB: At flimflammer aint gonna fit in at whatchajig.
ENG : That round piece won't fit in that square part.

Foot grips: *1. Shoes or boots.*
HB: I got sum new foot grips fer workin.
ENG: I picked up some new work boots today.

Furriner: *1. Someone not born in America.*
HB: Em furriners iz ever which way.
ENG: America is very ethnically diverse.

Fussi   n: *1. To be upset. 2. To complain.*
HB: Whatcha ya fussin fer, I needed ma tar fixed.
ENG: Honey I pawned your ring so I could get my tire fixed. Don't worry, it wasn't a real diamond anyway.

Gag a maggot: *1. Malodorous air. 2. An odor is choking you.*
HB: Heya darlin, ya lookin good but yer breath could gag a maggot.
ENG: Honey, you have morning breath.
Gander: *1. To look at or observe.*
HB: Hey ya wanna gander at the new park what I moved ma trailer to?
ENG: I moved my RV to a new park, want to check it out?

Geeonoweaheahh: *(GHEE-ON-OUW-A-HE-AH) 1. Please leave.*
HB: Geeonoweaheahh ya ransid polecat.
ENG: We are requesting your absence due to the malodorous air which

seems to linger around you.

Give out: *1. Stop working. 2. Not able to.*
HB: I reckon my back iz fixin ta give out.
ENG: I can't continue moving this furniture, my back hurts.

Gizzards: *1. Deep fried chicken guts. 2. Southern delicacy.*
HB: Em gizzards wuz good as a goats hoof on a hofbrow.
ENG: Honey, those chicken guts were pretty good.

Gumption: *1. Thinking about doing something.*
HB: I'ze gettin the gumption ta get some beer.
ENG: I'm thinking I need to do some shopping.

Hankerin: *1. To crave something.*
HB: I got me a hankerin fer sum possum and polk salad.
ENG: I could go for steak and salad tonight honey.

He'ahh: *1. Here.*
HB: Get up on ova he'ahh.
ENG: Come on over here.

Heap: *1. Large amount. 2. A lot.*
HB: I got me a heap a old tars out back.
ENG: I wish our neighbors would get rid of that pile of tires in their yard.

Hear tell: *1. Heard it through the grapevine. 2. Gossip.*
HB: I hear tell ya been buyin extra viddles from the milkman.
ENG: Are you having an affair with the milkman?

Heinz 57: *1. Dog with many mixed breeds.*
HB: At dog a yers is a heinz 57 aw ite.
ENG: The veterinarian doesn't even know what kind of a dog this is but he assured me it's not a monkey.

Here abouts: *1. Around here. 2. In this area.*
HB: Lotta good cookin here abouts.

ENG: There are many fine restaurants in this area.

Hi tail: *1. To leave or move quickly.*
HB: We bess hi tail it outta here cuz I got no money.
ENG: Darn, I have no cash, you want to try a dine and dash?

Hitched: *1. To become engaged or married.*
HB: Jim Bob got hitched up with Mary Ellen.
ENG: James recently became engaged to Mary.

Hog jowls: *1. Pork chops, pork steaks, ham hocks, pork by product etc.*
HB: Em aire hog jowls wuz better an a shin dig.
ENG: Those pork chops were excellent.

Holler: *1. To speak loudly. 2. To yell.*
HB: I had ta holler ta get em ta listen.
ENG: He was hard of hearing so I spoke loudly.

Hooten & hollerin: *1. Yelling and screaming.*
HB: He was a hooten & a hollerin.
ENG: He was yelling and screaming like a madman.

Hornswaggled: *1. To be deceived. 2. Cheated or scammed.*
HB: At aire map fella hornswaggled me.
ENG: This map to the movie stars homes only shows Rosie O'Donnels house. What a scam.

Iffin: *1. If.*
HB: Iffin y'ont ta.
ENG: If you would like to.

Iss: *1. This.*
HB: Iss yers?
ENG: Is this yours?

Issaway: *1. In this direction.*

HB: Move at aire over issaway.
ENG: Can you move the table towards me a few inches?

I'ze: *1. I am.*
HB: I'ze a talkin on the cb radia.
ENG: I am trying to communicate on this ancient low tech device.

Jaw flappin: *1. Talking. 2. Engaged in conversation.*
HB: Ed wuzza jaw flappin like a billy goat on a buckeye.
ENG: Edwin is long winded.

Jussi ***n:*** *1. Just in time (nick of time).*
HB: I made it to the crapper jussin time.
ENG: Lucky the restroom hade immediate seating available.

Jr.: *1. Insult. 2. Usually older man speaking to a younger man.*
HB: Don't talk back er all slap ya silly jr.
ENG: Show a little respect young man or I'll tap your mellon.

Kin folk: *1. Relatives.*
HB: I got kin folk up aire.
ENG: My sister lives in the mountains.

Knot: *1. Bump or contusion.*
HB: I'ze fixin ta knot yer head son.
ENG: I'm about ready to place a few contusions on your cranium.

Knuckle sandwic h: *1. To punch someone in the mouth.*
HB: Ya keepa messin with me all give ya a knuckle sandwich jr.
ENG: If you continue to bother me I will knock your bicuspids out you punk.

Lear ***n:*** *1. To teach someone.*
HB: I tried ta learn the kid but he's dumb as a box a rocks.
ENG: I think the new employee needs a little extra training.

Lick a sense: *1. Under educated. 2. Challenged.*

HB: At boy aint got a lick a sense.
ENG: That child is academically challenged.

Licki   n *: 1. To beat someone up. 2. To spank your child.*
HB: I'ze gonna give ya lickin ya aint never gonna ferget.
ENG: You're going on a time out little mister.

Like Ta*: 1. Almost.*
HB: I like ta got fard today.
ENG: I made a mistake at work today.

Lip Smakin*: 1. Extremely. 2. Hard to describe.*
HB: Em hog jowls was lip smakin good Velma darlin.
ENG: Your pork chops were delectable this evening honey.

Lollygaggin*: 1. To shirk your duties. 2. Avoiding responsibility.*
HB: Yer jussa lollygaggin around.
ENG: You need to quit messing around and finish your assignment.

Looksee*: 1. To visually observe.*
HB: I'll jus have me a little looksee.
ENG: Let me take a look at it.

Ma*: 1. Mother. 2. Other meanings include my, mine etc.*
HB: Ma is out fixin on the transmission.
ENG: Mother is very mechanically inclined.

Mall an are*: 1. Rate of speed.*
HB: I wuz comin off at hill at 90 mall an are.
ENG: I reached speeds around 90 miles per hour.

Mash: *1. To apply force.*
HB: Better mash on at peddle er else supper ill be cold.
ENG: We're late for dinner, drive a little faster.

Maters*: (may-ters) 1. Tomatoes.*
HB: Oze maters sho was tasty Ethyl.

ENG: Those tomatoes were at their peak of ripeness honey.

MeeMaw: *1. Grandmother.*
HB: How do MeMaw.
ENG: Hello Grandmother.

Mess: *1. A large amount.*
HB: I gots me a mess a viddles fer are cook out darlin.
ENG: I am having a barbeque and there is plenty of food.

Milkman: *1. Secret sex therapist.*
HB: Darlin, I'ze jussa thinkin eez kids a arz look just like the milkman.
ENG: Honey, I would like a divorce.

Mind: *1. To listen to. 2. Acknowledge.*
HB: Ya better pay sum mind ta yer boss son.
ENG: Follow instructions and listen to your boss son.

Muster: *1. To get or obtain.*
HB: I'ze a tryin ta muster up some gumption.
ENG: I need to get some more energy to finish this project.

Nader: *1. Tornado.*
HB: At aire nader cleaned out are whole town.
ENG: The local trailer park was leveled by a tornado.

Node: *1. Known, know, knew.*
HB: Dagburnit, I shoulda node ta set em varmit traps iss mornin.
ENG: Oh shoot, I forgot to set the mouse traps this morning.

No how: *1. Anyway. 2. Doesn't matter.*
HB: I didn't need at job no how.
ENG: I really didn't like that job anyway.

Notion: *1. Thinking about doing something.*
HB: Heya doll, I'ze gettin a notion ta grab ya up.
ENG: Honey, I think I really need a hug.

Nuthern: 1. Another one.
HB: Hun, kin I have a nuthern a oze dumplins?
ENG: Honey, may I have another dumpling?

Onry: (ON-REE) 1. Mean.
HB: At was an onry varmit.
ENG: That was an ill tempered rodent.

Otherin: 1. The other one(s).
HB: All take the otherins over aire.
ENG: I would prefer those over there.

Otta: 1. Should. 2. Used as a filler word.
HB: I reckon I otta get ta work now sweet pea.
ENG: Honey, I am leaving for work now.

Otthouse: 1. Outdoor bathroom. 2. Little shack with hole in ground.
HB: At otthouse is smellin a bit ripe ma.
ENG: Honey, I think it's time for some indoor plumbing.

Oughtnot: 1. Should not.
HB: You oughtnot oughta talk like at.
ENG: You shouldn't talk like that.

Oze: 1. Those.
HB: Oze kids a mine look juss like the milkman.
ENG: Honey, I would like to do a paternity test.

Pack: 1. To carry or move something.
HB: You reckon you can pack iss over yonder?
ENG: Can you move this over there?

Paw: 1. Father.
HB: Heya Paw, quick as ya finish up at 12 pack a beer wanna give me ma drivin lesson?
ENG: Is it safe to give me my driving lesson after drinking Father?

Pawpaw: *1. Grandfather.*
HB: How do Pawpaw.
ENG: Hello Grandfather.

Pay no mind: *1. Don't accept advice from. 2. Ignore.*
HB: Don't pay no mind ta him. He's dumb as a box a rocks.
ENG: Don't listen to him, he doesn't know what he is talking about.

Pester: *1. To bother or annoy.*
HB: Go an pester yer ma fer a spell.
*ENG: Honey, I think your mother is more qualified to answer that
question.*

Pin in the party hog: *1. To disrupt something. 2. Total chaos.*
HB: Elmer really stuck the pin in the party hog now.
ENG: Why did Elmer ruin your mothers fifth wedding?

Poke: *1. To pick on someone or something. 2. To make fun of.*
HB: Don't poke at Elly cuz she eats her buggers.
ENG: Don't make Fun of Elizabeth because she has a sinus infection.

Polecat: *1. Low life. 2. Trailer park trash.*
HB: Yer brother aint but a polecat LeAnn.
Eng: Honey, your brother needs to pull his life together.

Ponder, ponderi n: *1. To consider or think something over.*
HB: I'ze been ponderin bout it all fer five hole minutes Ethyl.
ENG: I've been thinking about your offer honey.

Posta: *(POSE-TA): 1. Supposed to.*
HB: I node I aint posta do at but aint nobody wuzza lookin.
ENG: It's not proper to urinate outdoors whether anyone is there or not.

Puke on a pork stick: *1. Compliment.*
HB: Yer ma's viddles wuz better an puke on a pork stick.

ENG: *Your Mother's cooking is better than a five star restaurant.*

Purtnea r: *1 Almost. 2. Nearly.*
HB: *I purtnear broke ma neck.*
ENG: *I slipped on the stairs and could have injured myself.*

Purty: *1. Pretty.*
HB: *Yer lookin mighty purty iss evenin sugar plum.*
ENG: *You look very pretty this evening honey.*

Rack: *1. Deer horns.*
HB: *Yer girl got a nice rack.*
ENG: *Your wife bagged a nice deer this year.*

Radia: *1. Radio.*
HB: *I got me a new radia fer listenin ta sum fiddle playin music.*
ENG: *I recently purchased a surround sound stereo to play my cd's.*

Reckon: *1. Suppose. 2. Think, hard to describe word.*
HB: *I don't ritely reckon it makes no matter no way.*
ENG: *I don't think it really matters.*

Rekalect: *1. To remember.*
HB: *I don't ritely rekalect.*
ENG: *I honestly do not remember.*

Ring a far: *(Ring of fire) 1. Severe burning sensation.*
HB: *Ma ring a far is flarin up doc.*
ENG: *I reached for the preparation "H" but accidentally used the Ben Gay.*

Ritely: *1. Honestly.*
HB: *I don't ritely rekalect..*
ENG: *I honestly do not remember.*

Rite quick: *1. Short period of time. 2. Do something quickly.*
HB: *I'ze gonna sit down rite quick.*

ENG: I'm going to sit down for a minute.

Roadkill: *1. Free dinner.*
HB: Good ya happened along at skunk fer supper darlin.
ENG: You hit WHAT with your car today?

Rub: *1. To pester or annoy.*
HB: Son, sumpin about ya juss rubs me the wrong way.
ENG: I don't know why but you annoy the heck out of me.

Ru   n: *1. To deliver. 2. Stop by.*
HB: At milkman run yet?
ENG: Has the milkman delivered our milk yet?

Sabbath: *1. Day of worship. Sunday. 2. Raceday.*
HB: Don't be gettin up on me darlin, em race cars is on and thays a drivin in a circle again. Get me a beer ya sweet little thing you.
ENG: Who watches this sport? I would need a twelve pack of beer and some stimulants to bear through this mindless entertainment.

Sap sucker *(suckin): 1. Some sort of low life loser.*
HB: Yer a sap suckin scalawag.
ENG: You're a pathetic loser.

Seed: *1. Seen. 2. Bear witness.*
HB: I seed a possum by the otthouse iss mornin.
ENG: There was a possum near our outdoor plumbing earlier.

Shake a stick at: *1. Something to do with counting things.*
HB: At computer fella has more money en ya can shake a stick at.
ENG: Mr. Gates has more money than you could ever count.

Shin dig: *1. Local gathering including, but not limited to, food and music.*
HB: Darlin, Rupert is puttin on a shim dig whatta make yer ear lobes wobble. Kin we go?
ENG: Honey, Rupert is having a block party and everyone is invited.

Would you like to attend?

Shotgun weddin: *1. Family gathering for an unplanned pregnancy.*
HB: Her Daddy's pickin me up fer a weddin I no nuttin about.
ENG: Her Father said he was picking me up for a blue steal wedding.

Sipher: *1. To recite.*
HB: Can ya sipher up summa em aire letters?
ENG: Can you recite the alphabet?

Six a eez er half dozen of the otherins: *1. Exactly the same.*
HB: Six a eez or half dozen of the otherins.
ENG: There is no difference, they are exactly the same.

Skeeters: *1. Mosquitoes.*
HB: eez he'ahh skeeters sho is thick iss evenin.
ENG: There are a lot of mosquitoes out here tonight.

Skwash *(squash): 1. To smash or squish something.*
HB: Yer gonna skwash yer finger.
ENG: That bearing press is going to smash your finger.

Skoolin: *1. To become educated.*
HB: Dorsey ill know, he gots some skoolin.
ENG: We should get advice from an expert.

Slim pickins: *1. Little choice.*
HB: Eez viddles iz slim pickins.
ENG: There is very little food left.

Slim ta none: *1. Odds are against you.*
HB: The odds a at happanin iz slim ta none, an slim just left town.
ENG: That will never happen.

Smack dab: *1. In the middle of. 2. Centered.*

HB: I wuz smack dab in at naders way.
ENG: That tornado was coming right toward us.

Smarts: 1. Painful.
HB: I stuck ma finger up in aire and it smarts a heap.
ENG: If you stick your finger in this machinery it will be very painful.

Spell: 1. Period of time.
HB: Aint seed Buford fer a spell.
ENG: Buford hasn't been around for a while.

Spittin Image: 1. To look or be exactly like someone or something.
HB: Son, yer the spittin image a at feller what gave us indoor plumbin juss before ya was born.
ENG: Honey, our son looks just like the contractor that worked on our house just before Billy was born. Want to tell me anything?

Study up on: 1. To think about.
HB: Let me study up on iss fer a spell.
ENG: Let me think about it for awhile.

Suga: 1. Like sugar without the "R". 2. Used as pet name for women.
HB: Heya suga plum, yer smellin rite purty.
ENG: Wow honey, I like your new perfume.

Switch: 1. Hand carved stick used to spank children.
HB: I'ze gonna cut me a hickory switch and lite a far on yer hide son.
ENG: I'm going to get a tree limb and spank your bottom.

Tar: 1. Tire.
HB: I got me a tar iss mornin.
ENG: I found a new tire reasonably priced on my way to work.

Tan: 1. To spank.

HB: Better shut that sassin er all tan yer hide.
ENG: Don't talk back to your Mother or I'll swat yer butt.

Tarnation: 1. ?
HB: What in tarnation er ya doin Cletus?
ENG: What in the world are you doing?

Tater: 1. Potato.
HB: I like em fried taters darlin.
ENG: Yes honey, I would enjoy some hash browns.

Tend: 1. To watch over.
HB: Ya better tend ta em youngsters.
ENG: Your children are out of control.

Tote: 1. To carry or move something.
HB: Ya reckon ya can tote iss over yonder?
ENG: Can you move this over there?

Tuckerd: 1. Tired. 2. Out of energy.
HB: I'ze about tuckerd out son.
ENG: I'm getting a little tired.

Up Aire: 1. Up there.
HB: I seed sumpin up aire.
ENG: There was a plane in the sky.

Ugly stick: 1. Measurement of beauty.
HB: Look like sum one beat her with an ugly stick.
ENG: I am not really attracted to her.

Uns: 1. One(s).
HB: Give me a handful a em uns over aire.
ENG: May I have 10 of those hard candies please?

Varmit: 1. Small animal. 2. Dog, rabbit, rodent etc.
HB: At was an onry varmit. Supper was fine ma.

ENG: That rat was ill tempered. What's for dinner?

Viddles: *1. Food, usually a meal.*
HB: Em was some rite fine viddles ma.
ENG: Dinner was delicious Mother.

Walleri n: *1: To wiggle or shake violently.*
HB: He wuzza wallerin around like a stuck pig.
ENG: When the police tazed that criminal he shook very violently.

Winder: *(WIND-ER) 1. Window.*
HB: At winder iz dirty as a polecat.
ENG: Honey, your windshield is filthy.

Whadja: *1.   Why did you. 2. What did you.*
HB: Whadja do at fer?
ENG: Why did you punch me in the eye?

Whall: *1. While.*
HB: Why dontcha stay fer a whall.
ENG: You just got here, stay for a while.

Whatchajig: *1.Word used to describe an unknown object.*
SEE "Flimflammer"

What not: *1. Everything else. 2. Lots of stuff.*
HB: They had viddles and what not.
ENG: They served dinner and dessert as well as beverages.

What yer at: *1. Where you are from or where you are.*
HB: Whats a name a at firm what yer at?
ENG: What is the name of that fly by night company you work for?

Whatta: *1. What would.*
HB: At picture show was spooky enough whatta make yer toe nails curl.
ENG: That movie was very scary.

Whittle: *1. To carve small wood with a pocket knife. 2. Hillbilly pastime.*
HB: I'ze gonna go downtown and whittle with the boys darlin.
ENG: Honey, I'm going to waste my time cutting sticks and making up lies
with my new buddies.

Wirehouse: *1. Warehouse.*
HB: I got me a job at the wirehouse.
ENG: I am gainfully employed at the warehouse.

Wore out: *1. Tired, out of energy.*
HB: Eatin at supper wore me out.
ENG: Eating that big dinner made me tired.

Yank: *1. To pull hard. 2 To remove or grab.*
HB: Heya doc, ya reckon ya kin yank iss tooth outta ma head fer me, it
hurts a heap.
ENG: Doctor, my tooth may have an abscess and need to be removed.

Yella: *1. Yellow. 2. Coward.*
HB1: Ya lookin right fine in at aire yella dress sweet cakes.
ENG1: That yellow dress is very becoming honey.
HB2: Yer a yella belly sap sucker Earl.
ENG2: You're a coward Earl.

Yer: *1. Your.*
HB: Yer sis is lookin rite fine tonight.
ENG: Your sisters prom dress is absolutely fabulous.

Y'all: *1. All of you.*
HB: How y'all doin?
ENG: Good morning, how are you?

Yicken: *1. Chicken.*
HB: I gots a hankerin fer yicken darlin.

ENG: May we have your delicious fried chicken tonight honey?

Y'ont: *1. Would you like. 2. Do you want.*
HB: Y'ont summa eze hog jowls?
ENG: Would you like a pork chop?

Yonder: *1. Over there.*
HB: Over yonder.
ENG: Over there.

Here are a few sayings I remember from my childhood

All slap ya so hard yer ma will feel it
All slap ya into the middle a next week
A rollin stone gathers no moss. (This makes sense)
Yer juss like ma wallet, always empty but I keep it anyway
Ats like leavin the fox ta watch the henhouse
All rattle yer teeth boy
I'ze gonna slap at guy silly
Yer barkin up the wrong tree
All knock ya fer a loop
All knock the far outta ya.
Ats like the pot callin the kettle black
He wuzza hootin & a hollerin
All wash yer mouth out with soap
I'm fixin ta give ya a knuckle sandwich

Here's ma knife, go cut a switch so I can whoop ya
I got a witch hazel bottle fulla whoop ass I'm fixin ta open on ya
Ya reap what ya sow
Want a trip to the woodshed son?
Iffin yer shoes a little tight, wear it anyway
Yer slower then a seven year itch
Open at fridge agin and ya gonna get frost bit
Ya keep poutin like at yer gonna step on yer lower lip
If Gods a willin and the creek don't rise

Here is a list of my favorite southern foods, highly recommended.

Grits
Catfish
Corn bread
Liver and onions
Crawdads (crawfish)
Louisiana Cajun
Fried zucchini
Fried potatoes
Homemade biscuits
Pinto beans with ham hawks
***real** southern pan fried chicken*
Polk salad (hard to find)
Milk gravy with biscuits

Chicken gizzards with gravy
Mashed potatos with skins on
Any gravy made from meat grease
Sausage gravy over eggs, toast or anything else

The Hillbilly Handbook of Etiquette Coming Soon!

Topics include
Personal hygiene
Dining out, shoes or not?
Teeth soaking, public or private?
Dating (relatives and or strangers)
Proper attire for any social event
Picking out the perfect trailer park

Printed in Great Britain
by Amazon